PAWNEE BILL'S HISTORIC WILD WEST

A Photo Documentary of the 1900-05 Show Tours

Allen L. Farnum

with the
Photos of Harry V. Bock (1865-1949)
Research assistance:
Martin G. Goebel

Schiffer Publishing Ltd

1469 Morstein Road, West Chester, Pennsylvania 19380

H

Dedication

With loving memories of
Dorothy Dallas Farnum
(1930-1989)

Front cover:
Arena and canvas poster, 1890-91. Circus World Museum.
Title page photo:
Cowboy poster, early 1890s. Circus World Museum.

Geronimo poster for the 1906 season—28" x 42" color
lithograph. Circus World Museum.

Copyright © 1992 by Allen Farnum
Library of Congress Catalog Number: 92-60904.

Printed in the United States of America.
ISBN: 0-88740-437-5

We are interested in hearing from authors with book ideas on related topics.

Published by Schiffer Publishing, Ltd.
1469 Morstein Road
West Chester, Pennsylvania 19380
Please write for a free catalog.
This book may be purchased from the publisher.
Please include $2.00 postage.
Try your bookstore first.

ACKNOWLEDGEMENTS

There are many people who have helped me over the past four years to make the dream of Harry Bock (publication of his photographs) finally come true. Some of those people who have my grateful appreciation include: Martin Goebel of Salem, Oregon, antique dealer/collector/appraiser, for providing the original motivation for this project, uncovering additional background, and finally finding a publisher; Jeff Briley, Historic Properties Manager, Pawnee Bill State Park (and museum), Pawnee, Oklahoma, owned by The State of Oklahoma Tourism and Recreation Department, for his encouragement early in my research and for providing assistance with their Pawnee Bill collection; Robert Parkinson, Director, and William McCarthy, Research Historian, Circus World Museum, Baraboo, Wisconsin, owned by the State Historical Society of Wisconsin, for invaluable help and access to the Pawnee Bill posters, route books, and a variety of Wild West printed material; Kenneth E. Farnum and Stanley R. Farnum of Great Barrington, Massachusetts, step-grandsons of Harry Bock, for the wealth of Bock history, photographs, and artifacts; nephew Daniel Bathurst for his original proof sheets of Harry Bock's negatives which inspired me to go back into a photo lab, recall some earlier training, and make up a complete set of 8 x 10 prints from all one hundred and fifty-five negatives; Morris Kagan of Encino, California, photojournalist, master lab technician, and friend, for expertly reprinting several of my mistakes which would otherwise be scattered throughout the book. To all of the above and many more who have helped along the way, my deep gratitude for your assistance in bringing this venture to a successful conclusion.

Pawnee Bill career poster, 1890-91. Circus World Museum.

Preface

Back around 1938 when I was a teenager growing up in Manchester, Vermont, my father, Lester Fayette Farnum, briefly showed me a collection of old 3" x 4" nitrate film negatives. They had been given to him by a local friend named Harry Bock who originally took the pictures in the early 1900s while on tour with what I always assumed was the "Buffalo Bill" Wild West show. Bock, already in his seventies, had asked my professional photographer father to eventually print and then somehow publish them since he'd never been able to do anything with the photos himself. My father stored the negatives away just as they'd been given to him. Apparently he just forgot all about them as he was working on a book of his own stories and art work, never published either. When I found them among Dad's things in 1970, following his death at age ninety, I glanced briefly at them and filed them away again—just another set of old negatives.

In 1984, when I retired from NBC-TV in Los Angeles and we moved to Oregon, I ran across the negatives again while sorting and packing, but they still remained unidentified. When I mentioned "historical negatives" in 1988 to a local antique dealer, he encouraged me to find out what I really had. They turned out to be a very unique photo chronology of one hundred fifty-five, perfectly preserved negatives of Pawnee Bill's Wild West show on the road from 1900 to 1905. It was truly a remarkable amateur photographer's time capsule of one era of early American history—wagons, livestock, buffalo, equipment, cowboys, cowgirls, Indians, tents, midway crowds—almost everything and everybody in the show had been documented.

Strangely enough, there was not one single image of Pawnee Bill himself in Harry Bock's negative collection. Because it's difficult to imagine such a thorough coverage of the Wild West show without Pawnee Bill being included, I can only guess that, for some reason, they were removed right after Bock took the original pictures. For filing simplification, I chose to keep and use Bock's numbers for all his negatives, even though someone has inked other numbers that don't match on a few. The captions (except the portions in Italics) are also Bock's original word for word on all his photographs. The author's captions are on most other credited prints or material.

Bock had filed each negative by inserting it between the pages of a diary with name, date, and location, with a few tucked into old envelope halves. Fortunately this was prior to acidic paper, so practically all the negatives are as good as new—almost ninety years later. Cowboy/carpenter/photographer/minister Harry Bock finally gets his wish!

Contents

May Lillie poster, 1893-94. Circus World Museum.

Paris World's Fair poster, 1897-98. Circus World Museum.

Pawnee Bill: Major Gordon W. Lillie

Gordon William Lillie—Wild West showman, buffalo hunter, plains scout, cowboy, white chief of the Pawnees, land boomer, oilman, banker, conservationist—was born on February 14, 1860 in Bloomington, Illinois. He was the oldest of four children whose family owned and operated a successful steam powered flour mill. As a boy, Gordon was fascinated by the frontier stories of cousins and avidly read the Ned Buntline adventures about war, Indians, and the western plains. Indeed, he first became acquainted with the exploits of Buffalo Bill Cody by reading about him.

When Gordon was thirteen, his dream to go west was made possible by an unforseen accident. The flour mill burned and the family moved by covered wagon to Wellington, Kansas to start all over again. Even though his parents wanted Gordon to become a teacher, his heart was further out on the unexplored prairie and the frontier activity. Various Indian tribes passed through the area near where he lived on their way south to resettlement areas in the Indian Territory. This was where Gordon first became friends with the Pawnee.

The urge to explore on his own finally was realized, but Gordon soon learned just how rough the booming town of Wichita could be. At age fifteen, he was forced into a gun battle and had to kill a man in self-defense. That incident was enough to head him south into the Indian Territory to find his Pawnee friend, Black Hawk. Since young Gordon had already learned some respect for the Pawnee values and traditions, he was readily accepted at the Pawnee Agency. He spent the next year living among the Indians, discovering a new way of life in the teachings of the tribal elders. He also became friends with Major William Bishop, the Indian agent who was responsible for bringing the Pawnees into the Territory.

Gordon learned the Pawnee language, went buffalo hunting, and watched his Pawnee friends go off to fight the Cheyenne when they were recruited by the U.S. Government. Later he spent a year and a half along the Arkansas River, fur trapping in the company of an Indian trader called Trapper Tom. In 1878 he helped his Pawnee friends recover horses stolen by marauding Comanches and was rewarded with the title of "White Chief of the Pawnees." A new Indian agent made Gordon the official interpreter and he eventually wound up teaching the Pawnees at the Agency school. That's where he picked up the name "Pawnee Bill." In the summer of 1881, Gordon was fired from the teaching job after he knocked down a new and jealous superintendent.

Following this period, Lillie worked as a wagon team driver in the Cherokee Outlet and, as a cowboy, was wounded by rustlers. In 1883, he had his first contact with the Boomers, those farmers and their families who were waiting in Caldwell, Kansas for the unclaimed lands in the Indian Territory to open up for settlement. That vast area was leased to cattle barons for grazing rights while the homesteaders were being kept out by military force. After he became friends with the Boomer leader, David Payne, what Gordon saw and heard in Kansas would greatly influence the action he would later take in 1889.

At this point, in 1883, Buffalo Bill Cody was about to enter Lillie's life in a way that would make them life-long friends. The very first Wild West show by Cody was set to make its debut in Omaha and Gordon was officially assigned by the Indian Commissioner to take charge of the Pawnees who had been hired to appear in it. The show was a sell-out success all across the country with its cowboys, Indians, trick riders, marksmen, wild steers, buffalo, and stagecoach pursuit. When the show hit Philadelphia, love hit Gordon Lillie in the form of a city-bred, Smith College girl named May Manning. At the end of the show season, Gordon returned to the cattle ranch he now owned in Medicine Lodge, Kansas while he and May kept a steady flow of letters going between them.

The next season Gordon/Pawnee Bill took his Pawnee Indians back on Buffalo Bill's Wild West tour and when the show hit Philadelphia again, he proposed to May. Against her socially prominent mother's wishes, May agreed to become his future bride. About midway through the tour, he learned of the death of his Boomer friend David Payne and that the homesteaders had been forcefully ejected by the Army for trying to move onto the public domain lands of the Indian Territory. All efforts at opening up the lands for settlement were hopelessly ensnared in political controversy and cattlemen's favoritism. Pawnee Bill returned to his ranch, but now with a new idea implanted in his mind. Why not a Wild West show of his own?

May Manning and Gordon W. Lillie were married August 31, 1886 and the Quaker society girl went west to Kansas and the open plains. About a year later their six week old son died and complications prevented May from having any more children. From that day on, she threw herself into learning how to ride, rope, and shoot like a real cowgirl. Sidesaddle on a running horse, she became a sensational marksman.

Pawnee Bill's Wild West hit the road in the spring of 1888. It starred May Lillie, Trapper Tom, brother Al Lillie, Indians from five different tribes, 165 people, 165 animals, and Pawnee Bill himself. It was a huge success at first, probably because Buffalo Bill's Wild West was in England and famed sharpshooter Annie Oakley was free to join the show for a few months. Unfortunately that first season ended with bad weather, Buffalo Bill's return, and such slow business that the show equipment and stock were attached in Maryland for non-payment of debts.

About this time the pressure on Washington from the railroads and various cities in Kansas to open up the Oklahoma lands had forced a turning point. Pawnee Bill was asked to come back west and lead the Boomer movement while they were waiting for final approval to move in and settle on the unclaimed Indian Territories. With enough national newspaper publicity, public opinion, and political pressure, a bill was finally signed into law. On April 22, 1889, Pawnee Bill, on horseback, personally led a group of about 3500 settlers on the run into Oklahoma and overnight found himself a national hero.

The publicity he had gained now made it much easier for Pawnee Bill to reorganize his show. It was renamed "Pawnee Bill's Historical Wild West, Indian Museum, and Encampment". It was also bigger, better, and much more successful this time around. He toured the U.S. and Canada for three years, adding the Mexican Hippodrome and chariot races in 1893. That was also the year that the Cherokee Outlet in Oklahoma was opened to settlement. Pawnee Bill and his family bought lots around the booming town of Pawnee and from that time he made the area his home.

Movie poster from one of the several serial films about Pawnee Bill's real and imagined exploits—circa 1930s. Pawnee Bill Museum.

Pawnee Bill around 1900 in buckskin clothes. Pawnee Bill Museum.

Indian camp poster, 1890-1892. Circus World Museum.

In 1894 Pawnee Bill's Wild West appeared at the World's Fair in Belgium, but business dropped off so much toward the end of the tour that his equipment and stock were again confiscated for non-payment of expenses. This time, a local businessman bailed him out and he then toured Holland and France, but still returned to the U.S. essentially without operating capital. He rebuilt his wagons on borrowed funds and the following year rapidly recouped his losses once he was back on the road.

"Mexican Joe", Jose Barrera, rope artist and trick rider from San Antonio, joined the Wild West for the 1898 tour, was granted top billing, and probably became the most permanent cowboy in the organization. In the later years, Mexican Joe became ranch foreman when Pawnee Bill finally retired to his property in Pawnee. Sometime during this period, the show's advance men began using the title "Colonel" on Gordon W. Lillie's colorful lithographed advertising. It stuck with him. Also this was about the time that the fiction writers of the period picked up on the real and imaginary exploits of Pawnee Bill and, like his boyhood hero Buffalo Bill Cody, he became a real-life frontier hero to other people.

During the next few years Pawnee Bill split his time into two different life styles. Relaxed winters in Pawnee were spent with banking, conventional business, and politics. The balance of the year under the big top involved long hours, daily train travel, and a return to the earlier cowboy life. His astute investments helped Pawnee Bill become prosperous. During this same era, Buffalo Bill, who was not a good businessman, threw his money around on many unwise ventures and also had a drinking problem.

Even when there were conflicts between them, there was enough room in the country so that the two biggest Wild West shows did not infringe too much on each other's territories. With their success came an influx of other Wild West shows like wild mushrooms popping up through buffalo chips after the spring rains on the prairie. At least thirty competitors galloped on the scene and just as rapidly faded into the dust during those early 1900s. Among them: Indian Bill's Wild West, Luella Forepaugh-Fish Wild West, Cole Younger-Frank James Wild West, Colonel Jack's Wild West, Colonel Cummings Indian Congress and Life on the Plains, Wild Bill's Wild West, Hulberg's Wild West and Congress of the Nations of the World, Tiger Bill's Wild West, and Colonel Zack Mulhall's Wild West. From 1883 into the 1930s there were well over one hundred Wild West shows, though they were occasionally the same show with a new name, new owners, or a different partner.

Pawnee Bill by now had accumulated a large herd of buffalo at his Blue Hawk Peak ranch in Pawnee. He had long been aware of the fast disappearance of the great plains herds of buffalo, so he became an active conservationist in buffalo preservation on a national level. His efforts to save the few buffalo still surviving eventually paid off.

In 1904 Pawnee Bill added the name "The Great Far East" to his show when he introduced exotic foreign acts which had never been seen before in this country. His show was also beginning to run into booking problems against the Barnum and Bailey Circus and the Ringling Brothers organization. Colonel Cody over the years had frequently switched partners because of his repeated personal financial problems. In 1908 Pawnee Bill unexpectedly bought out the James Bailey interest in the Buffalo Bill Wild West. From that point on May Lillie refused to ever appear with "Buffalo Bill's Wild West and Pawnee Bill's Great Far East", as it was now called. She felt it was a huge mistake to make such a gamble when their own show was doing so well by itself.

Pawnee Bill in his early thirties wearing his favorite western outfit. Pawnee Bill Museum.

May Lillie and Pawnee Bill as they posed in an early advertisement for Pawnee Bill's Wild West. Pawnee Bill Museum.

The combined show was to last for only five years. Buffalo Bill, through bad management and his penchant for reckless investments, soon forfeited his financial interest in the show back to the Baileys. In order to salvage what he could, Pawnee Bill paid off Cody's outstanding debts and became sole owner of the show. Partly because of sentiment and also because of generosity Pawnee Bill then deeded a half interest in the show right back to Buffalo Bill with the condition that it eventually be repaid out of Cody's future earnings. It didn't quite work out that way.

Buffalo Bill's Wild West and Pawnee Bill's Great Far East embarked on a three year "Farewell to Colonel Cody" tour which was to be completed in 1912. However, a one year ill-planned extension ended in disaster in July of 1913. Buffalo Bill, always in debt and sinking deeper, had secretly borrowed more money against the show. To compound the problems, he was also planning to leave the Two Bills show for the Sells-Floto Circus owned by Denver Post proprietor Harry Tamen. In addition, the unfavorable weather had so reduced gate receipts that the unpaid bills for the daily operating expenses were already into thousands of dollars. Combined with the debts, outside greed and jealousy plus political maneuvering forced the last great Wild West show into bankruptcy. All the stock, wagons, tents, equipment, everything ended up on the auctioneer's block in Denver, in September, 1913. Pawnee Bill went home with nothing but his saddle and one trunk.

The show could have been saved one more time by Pawnee Bill since he had the resources, but he was tired of Buffalo Bill's financial shenanigans. Besides he now had a magnificent new ranch house and May Lillie was waiting in Pawnee.

Colonel William F. Cody returned to North Platte until it was time for him to join the Sells-Floto Circus. He travelled with them for only one year, and after other unsuccessful attempts at reviving a Wild West show, died in Colorado on January 10, 1917 at the age of seventy-one.

Between oil, banking, and real estate, Pawnee Bill and May were financially secure for the rest of their lives. Their ranch became a gathering spot for famous people from around the world. Pawnee Bill now became active in many civic and charitable organizations. He and May had finally found time for a child and adopted a baby boy in 1916. However Billy was killed in an accident at the ranch when he was only nine years old. By 1930 Lillie had pioneered the construction nearby of Old Town and an Indian trading post in an effort to retain some of the flavor of the old west. Pawnee Bill and May celebrated their fiftieth wedding anniversary at a special celebration in their honor in Taos, New Mexico in August of 1936. Two weeks later May was fatally injured in an auto accident while Pawnee Bill was driving home from Tulsa. She died on September 14. Major Gordon W. Lillie/Pawnee Bill lived another active, but peaceful six years on the ranch until his death on February 3, 1942 at age 82.

With the exception of Old Town which burned to the ground in 1939, all of the original ranch buildings, their furnishings, and most of the Lillie's imported European items have been preserved. The Pawnee Bill Museum and Ranch at Blue Hawk Peak is now a historical research center and recreational facility owned and operated by the State of Oklahoma, Department of Parks and Recreation. Even now Pawnee Bill's dream to educate and entertain lingers on!

One example of a Pawnee Bill eight-sheet lithograph poster, about 7 x 9 feet, originally done in brilliant colors. Pawnee Bill Museum.

A young May Lillie as she first appeared with Pawnee Bill's wild west. Pawnee Bill Museum.

1930 flyer from the Old Town and Trading Post. It burned to the ground in 1939. Kenneth Farnum.

Pawnee Bill and May's 50th wedding anniversary—reproduced from an old newspaper. She was killed in an auto accident two weeks later. Kenneth Farnum.

Buffalo Bill Cody in front of log cabin on Pawnee Bill's buffalo ranch, Pawnee, Oklahoma, December 22, 1910. Kenneth Farnum.

15

Ranch foreman Mexican Joe with Pawnee Bill at the ranch house in the mid-1930s. Pawnee Bill Museum.

Pawnee Bill's Ranch House as it looks today in Pawnee, Oklahoma.

Pawnee Bill—Prophet in His Home Town

PAWNEE, Okla., Sept. 8, 1933.—Disproving the old time saga that a man is never a prophet in his home town the Mayor and City Council of Pawnee gave a surprise banquet at Pawnee, Thursday night, September 7, at which time they presented a scroll resolution embodying the sentiments of the community and the county and declaring Major Gordon W. Lillie to be the first citizen of Pawnee and the State of Oklahoma.

Commending Major Lillie on his half century of untiring labor the City Attorney of Pawnee, the Honorable Emerson R. Phillips, stressed the fact that the City was proud to pay tribute to the last of the five great historical figures, who planned and were responsible for the opening of Oklahoma and the Cherokee Strip.

Clipping from an Oklahoma newspaper—September 1933. Pawnee Bill Museum.

The "Buckskin Harry" Story

Harry Valentine Bock was born in Hazelton, Pennsylvania on July 17, 1865. His father, Valentine, born in Germany, married a Pennsylvania girl whose parents also had emigrated to the United States from Germany. Harry was the oldest of five children which included a brother Franklin (1869-1935) who became a doctor, and sisters Sarah Malinda (Everett), Adeline Elizabeth (1874-?), and Mary Angeline who died at age eight. During 1868 the family moved to the Boston area where the rest of the children were born, went to school, and grew up.

By the time Harry was a teenager, he was not only handy with tools but good enough with horses to join the movement westward as a cowboy. Around 1882 he made it all the way to Wyoming where he worked for some time as a government scout or agent, according to old family letters. During these early frontier days, he became known as "Buckskin Harry" and probably struck up the beginning of his friendship with Pawnee Bill. He was also attached to the Army at one period, but the military records are not very clear on this area of his life. In 1886, the year he turned twenty-one, Harry did return to Boston just long enough to marry his childhood sweetheart, Paulina Anne Mohr, daughter of another emigrated German family. Whether she ever traveled with Harry during the following years is not a matter of record, but with one son after another it's obvious he found time to regularly return home.

Beginning in 1892, Harry joined Pawnee Bill's Wild West as a cowboy and doubled as a carpenter. As his cowboy activities were gradually phased out, he spent more and more of his time over the next sixteen years designing, building, and repairing special circus wagons whenever the show ended up in winter quarters. Several examples of his work still exist in the show pictures he took. He and Pawnee Bill established a life-long friendship that endured until Pawnee Bill's death.

On page 16 of the Official Pawnee Bill Route Book published at the end of the 1898 season, Harry Bock is listed as a carpenter under the Mechanical Department. On his original undated picture #44, Bock however lists himself as "Master Mechanic" even though there is no official record of him working on the road as such in any earlier or later shows. According to his hand written notes with the negative collection, the pictures were dated from 1900 to 1905. That would indicate that he traveled with the show again at some point but not in any performing capacity. Since he only worked in the winter quarters shop during those years, his name would not show up in any other route books. Among his notes, those for negative #30 credit Harry with building a large prairie schooner in winter quarters at Carnegie, Pennsylvania for the 1901-1902 season.

Only one picture exists of a young Bock in western gear on horseback with a Winchester rifle under his arm, probably taken before he joined Pawnee Bill. A page by page reading of the 1898 route book indicates that "Buckskin Harry" worked in at least six of the acts where he doubled as a cowboy, trick roper, and team driver. Interestingly enough, most

Buckskin Harry
Hat Creek   Wyoming

"Buckskin Harry" Bock as he looked in 1885-86 before joining Pawnee Bill's Wild West. Lester Farnum.

Buckskin Harry, Hat Creek, Wyoming. "This was taken in 1885. My first trip back from the West." Kenneth Farnum.

all of the people and acts that Harry photographed were not listed on that 1898 Pawnee Bill Wild West roster. It's easy to speculate that his titles and dates were written up some years later as he tried to recall who, when, and where. That could account for some of the obvious discrepancies which have shown up in his written material.

Bock was so captivated by the Wild West show idea and his two heroes (Buffalo Bill and Pawnee Bill) that in 1900 he temporarily changed his name to "Buckskin Bill" and proceeded to form his own small Wild West show. It was less than a roaring success even if Harry did use the standard advertising and equipment. He was bankrupt within a year.

A major turning point in Bock's life took place in 1903 while at the Carnegie winter quarters: Harry was formally baptized into the Southern Baptist Convention. For the next five years, he seriously pursued theological studies between more carpentering, less cowboying, and trips back to Manchester, Vermont where most of his relatives now lived. His father died in 1905, but his mother still ran the farm they owned up there in the Green Mountains and his two sisters were nearby. Harry's own family by now had grown to include three sons—Robert, Frank, and Harry, Jr.

Buckskin Harry ended his association with Pawnee Bill's Wild West in 1908. Needless to say, it was by no means the end of his personal friendship with Gordon Lillie. Harry by now had completed enough basic theology to be assigned as a Southern Baptist Missionary. His very first mission was to the Pawnee Indians in Pawnee, Oklahoma which co-incidentally was also the location of Pawnee Bill's ranch and buffalo herd. Certainly Reverend Bock's beginning assignment, which was to extend over the next fourteen years, was based on more than chance. Earlier in that same year, the Bocks had purchased a comfortable house in Manchester which remained as the home to return to as often as possible. However, this time Harry's wife and sons moved with him to the Pawnee Reservation to start this new adventure. Harry threw himself completely into the Indian missionary work as evidenced by stories about him in the official Southern Baptist publications of that period. At a later date he worked with the nearby Otoe Tribe in addition to his continuing efforts with the Pawnee.

In an effort to supplement the meager income of an Indian missionary, the Reverend Bock still kept his skilled hands busy in the carpenter field. In the 1910 construction photographs of Pawnee Bill's big new stone ranch house, Harry is plainly identified among the working men in at least two of the pictures. In his own handwriting on the reverse side, he has written "Harry Bock—Architect/Builder" although existing Pawnee Bill biographies do not give him any credit as such.

This was also the year that Harry's mother became seriously ill and he made a trip to the family farm back in the Green Mountains. He, his mother Angeline, and his spinster sister Adeline were the only Bock family members in Manchester to show up in the 1910 census of Vermont. His mother unfortunately only lived another two years.

Before many years had gone by, each of the three Bock sons had struck out on his own. Harry Junior was killed in France in World War I and Robert moved to El Dorado, Arkansas. Frank was the only one to follow in his father's footsteps by also becoming a minister, ending up in Luke City, Nebraska.

By 1923 the Reverend Harry Bock had completed his assignment with the Pawnee Indian Baptist Mission, so he and Paulina left Oklahoma, permanently moving back to Manchester. This time they moved into a new house that Harry had

46. Mechanical dept. 1901-03

Enlargement of Harry Bock from 1903 photograph. He listed himself as "Master Mechanic" with Pawnee Bill Wild West at that time.

20

One of Buckskin Bill's Wild West wagons—1901. Kenneth Farnum

built mostly by himself. There in Vermont, he worked locally for the next few years as a building and construction carpenter. He held religious meetings at home on occasion, but during this time of his life Bock maintained no formal church affiliation. He also took up model making, becoming a skilled craftsman of ships and wagons.

In March of 1929 Bock's wife Paulina died very suddenly at age sixty-two while they were at home in Manchester. By the end of the year, Harry, who was now sixty-four, was married for a second time to a charming widow named Grace May Blake Farnum. She was twelve years younger than he and had three grown sons of her own: Wilson, Roy, and Kingsley Farnum.

There are still a few old timers back in the Green Mountain state that remember Harry Bock as a short, slightly built, quiet man with a droopy mustache who lived a typical small town life as he grew older. Apparently very few local people were ever aware of his early cowboy or Wild West show days. Woodworking, model making, and religion were a long way from his earlier days of travel and frontier adventure.

Old friend Pawnee Bill never forgot "Buckskin Harry" as the years passed them by. In addition to annual Christmas cards, one wishful letter written in 1933 by Pawnee Bill was to ask Harry if he'd still be interested in building a series of show wagons for a proposed new Wild West to appear at the upcoming Chicago World's Fair. There is no record of it ever happening.

Apparently a new wife added a little inspiration to Harry's life. Beginning in 1933, the Rev. Bock returned to ministering on a regular basis as pastor of the Center White Creek Baptist Church. There was only one drawback. The church was many miles away from Manchester across the state line in New York. Still Harry made that long drive for almost six years just so he could have his own church again.

As he got older, the travel time and distance involved forced the Reverend Bock to make a new decision and yet another housing change. In 1938 he finally sold the house in Manchester and moved into New York state so he would be convenient to the church. By 1940 he was offered another pastor's position at the nearby Lebanon Springs Baptist Church where he remained for the next two years. In 1944 Harry made one more move to the First Baptist Church of Athens, New York—his last assignment until official retirement five years later in 1949.

It seems strange indeed that fate should strike similar tragic blows to two old friends in their senior years. Pawnee Bill's wife had been killed in an auto accident back in 1936 as they was driving home from Tulsa. Fortunately Major Lillie survived his injuries. In the fall of 1949 the Reverend Harry Bock and his wife were driving to their new retirement home across the Hudson River in Massachusetts when he was fatally injured by a careless young driver on a winding mountain road. Buckskin Harry died October 13 at age eighty-four. His wife May never recovered from her injuries and died almost exactly one year later.

Little did Harry Bock know that his foresighted venture into photography would live on as an excellent example of historical documentation of a very unique piece of Americana—the Wild West show.

Another of Buckskin Bill's wagons—1901. Kenneth Farnum

BURLINGTON, WIS.

MONDAY

JULY 29

Two Performances, 2 p. m. 8 p. m. Rain or Shine.

The same Magnificent Exhibition that Delighted Thousands in St. Louis, Indianapolis, Detroit, Columbus, Memphis and other large cities.

COL. V. F. CODY.

BUCKSKIN BILL'S

REALISTIC

WILD WEST!

GRAND

Military Tournament and Rough Riders of the World

Purely Educational, Genuinely Historical, Delightfully Amusing. A Grand Inspiring Exhibition, consisting of Cow Boys, Indians, Mexicans, Arabs, Cossacks, United States, English, German and French Cavalrymen, Roosevelt's Rough Riders and Battery of Light Artillery.

Requiring 1000 Men and Horses.

BUCKSKIN BILL

Among the many features of this Mammoth Exhibition will be Feats of Marksmanship, introducing Buckskin Bill, who will appear at each performance day and night, and give his wonderful exhibition of shooting from horse back at full speed, also a score of Male and Female Crackshots of the World in plain and fancy shooting.

Wild Broncos, a Herd of Buffalo and Texas Steers

FREE STREET PARADE!

AT 10 a. m.

Cow Boy Band of Fifty Famous Musicians.

Two Exhibitions Daily, Rain or Shine. Afternoon at 2, Night at 8. Doors open one hour earlier. 1901

Buckskin Bill generic advertisement for a show in Burlington, Wisconsin on July 29, 1901—he didn't make it. Circus World Museum.

Bill Woodcock's Circus Letterheads

THE LARGEST AND BEST WILD WEST EXHIBITION NOW IN AMERICA.

H. E. ALLOTT, MANAGER.

HARRY W. SEMON, GEN'L AGENT. AND RAIL ROAD CONTRACTOR.

PERMANENT ADDRESS. 206 WEST ADAMS ST. CHICAGO, ILL.

BUCKSKIN BILL'S CONSOLIDATED WILD WEST SHOWS.

A HERD OF GENUINE FULL BLOODED BUFFALOES, WILD BEASTS, ELEPHANTS, CAMELS, ELK AND MEXICAN BULLS, COWBOYS, COWGIRLS, SCOUTS, INDIANS, SQUAWS, PAPOOSES, COSSACKS. SPECTACULAR ILLUSTRATIONS OF PAST WESTERN HISTORICAL FACTS, AND THE ONLY ORIGINAL WORLD'S FAMOUS AMERICAN STREATOR ZOUAVES. 1901

BUCKSKIN BILL'S REALISTIC WILD WEST.

BUCKSKIN BILL. RED BLANKET.

A HERD OF GENUINE FULL BLOODED BUFFALOES, CONGRESS OF COWBOYS, COTERIE OF INDIANS, ROUGH RIDERS, GAUCHOS AND REAL RACING HIPPODROME.

H. E. ALLOTT, MANAGER. HARRY W. SEMON, GEN'L AGENT.

The Erie Lithograph Co., is credited with naming a number of circuses, because of having litho paper on the shelf, with a given title.

The Erie company had many stock designs of letterpaper, heralds and couriers, illustrations from one show's advertising could often be seen as a part of material used by another show.

A good example of the rehashing of letterhead designs is shown here. The top letterhead is identical to the 1903 Luella Forepaugh Fish Wild West design, except for the name. The 1904 Buckskin Bill paper is printed in bright red, outlined in gold. The three illustrations are in black.

The lower letterhead is printed in blue and gold, with illustrations in blown. The year of the lower sheet may also have been 1904.

1904 Buckskin Bill letterhead. The show folded in 1901 but his name lived on in print. Circus World Museum.

Buckskin Bill "review" in Beloit, Wisconsin, Daily Free Press of July 27, 1901. Circus World Museum.

CROWD WAS DISAPPOINTED

BUCKSKIN BILL'S CIRCUS FAILS TO SHOW UP.

People Came to Town From Every Direction but the Imitation of Buffalo Bill's Show Came to Grief in an Illinois Town and "Busted."

SHOW WAS THE RANKEST KIND OF A SNIDE ANYWAY.

The streets were crowded to-day with people who came from every direction to see Buckskin Bill's Wild West show. But they were doomed to disappointment, for the celebrated galaxy of bright and particular stars failed to appear, and a dispatch in a metropolitan paper says it came to an ignominious end down at Sandwich, Ill. The show was billed at Sycamore, Ill., yesterday and failed to appear there, also. Three members of the cowboy band of the show and whose homes are in Whitewater are said to have passed through Beloit last night on their way home and gave out the statement that the show had "busted."

The crowd was loth to leave the street in spite of the statement of "no show" given out up and down the streets by the police and others. They hung on to the forlorn hope that maybe by some magic "hokus pokus" the grand cavalcade would yet appear. As the dinner hour approached, however, and no parade showed up, the fact slowly dawned on the crowd that they had been swindled, by whom they knew not, being about as much inclined to hold the police, who acquainted them with the facts, responsible as the show itself. One gay sport from the rural district with his coat lapels covered with gaudy ribbons and badges was heard to remark, *sotto voce:* "Dol blast the dod rotted show to be ding; I just knew they wouldn't come, and I'll be derned if I ever go to another one!" But he'll be right on hand the very next time circus day comes, just the same.

It is a wonder this "Buckskin Bill" combination hasn't hit the earth ere this, for of all the brazen imitations ever sprung, it was the worst. That it was a snide was perfectly plain to those who noticed the posters and lithographs and advertising matter generally. All was in direct imitation of the paper of the famous old scout, Buffalo Bill, who is one of nature's noblemen. Even the name was copied as near as possible. "Buckskin" said his name was Col. V. F. Cody, thus differing from Col. W. F. Cody in only one initial. Oh, "Buckskin Bill," if we ever get hold of you"

Buckskin Bill and his rough riders failed to materialize in Stoughton last Tuesday, as advertised. The printers, livery men and hotel men, each with an order "good at the ticket-wagon," are the only sufferers. The aggregation went to pieces about two weeks ago.

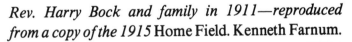

On the back is written: "Harry Bock and James Warren in Carnegie, Penna 1904. Harry baptized there Mar. 3, 1904. James saved in New York State 1906." Kenneth Farnum.

Rev. Harry Bock and family in 1911—reproduced from a copy of the 1915 Home Field. Kenneth Farnum.

Deacons with their wives, missionary, Harry Bock, and interpreter, David Gillingham, of the Pawnee Indian Baptist Church, Pawnee, Oklahoma, Dec 23, 1911. Lester Farnum.

25

Rev. Harry Bock baptizing oldest Otoe Indian in 1915 at the Mission in Pawnee. Kenneth Farnum.

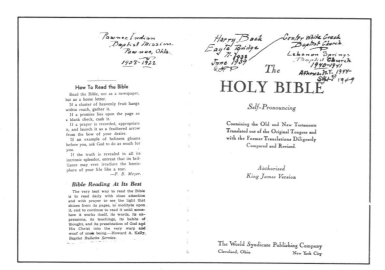

Bock bible title page, with his handwritten record of churches that he served in from 1908 to 1949. Kenneth Farnum.

Rev. Harry Bock with Sitting Bull on the cover of Home Field, *April, 1915. It's really a composite photo and never happened. Kenneth Farnum.*

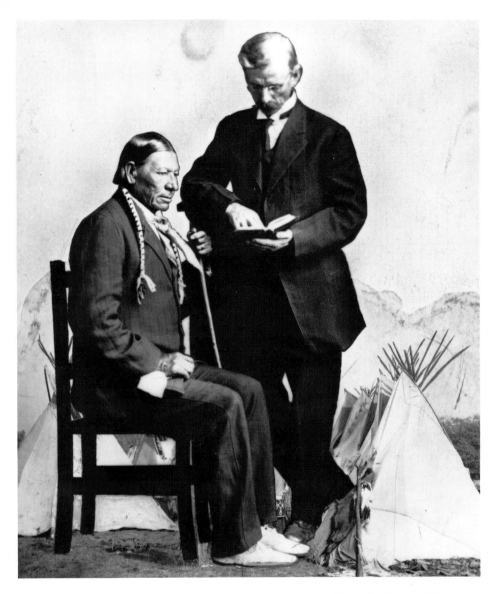

Bock and Bull. The full-sized faked picture from the Lester Farnum files in Vermont. Sitting Bull died in 1890.

Contents page of the April, 1915 Home Field *with two articles by the Reverend Harry Bock.* Kenneth Farnum

THE HOME FIELD

PUBLISHED BY THE

HOME MISSION BOARD OF THE SOUTHERN BAPTIST CONVENTION

SUBSCRIPTION PRICE - 35 CENTS PER YEAR.

1004-5-6-7-8-9-10 HEALEY BUILDING. ATLANTA. GA.

VICTOR I. MASTERS, Editor.   M. M. WELCH, Business Manager.

CONTENTS FOR APRIL, 1915.

THE HOME FIELD is the Home Mission Organ of the Southern Baptist Convention. Published monthly.

SUBSCRIPTION PRICE, 35 cents per year in advance; clubs of five or more, 25 cents each.

CHANGE OF ADDRESS. Requests for change of address must state old and new addresses, and reach this office not later than the 19th of the month preceding the date upon which it is desired to have the change made. Where this notification does not reach us by the date indicated, subscribers may have the magazine forwarded by sending two cents to the postmaster at the old address.

ADVERTISING. A limited amount of space is available for advertising purposes. The character of advertising will be restricted within definite limits, and no advertisements of any person, firm or corporation, nor of any business or commodity not known to be responsible and reputable, will be accepted for publication. For rates address M. M. WELCH, Business Manager, Atlanta, Ga., or FRED D. YATES, Eastern Representative, 150 Nassau Street, New York.

CORRESPONDENCE AND REMITTANCES should be addressed to THE HOME FIELD, 1004 Healey Building, Atlanta, Georgia.

Entered at the Post Office in Atlanta, Ga., for Transmission at Second-Class Rate.

Model of prairie schooner built by Harry Bock in 1931. Lester Farnum.

PAWNEE BILL'S OLDTOWN

PAWNEE ⚥ OKLAHOMA

GORDON WM. LILLIE
"PAWNEE BILL"

December 23, 1933.

Dear Harry:

There is an awfully good chance that I will put on the biggest Wild West Show at the World's Fair in Chicago that has ever been given in the United States. If I do I should like very much to have you come on and build me two or three prairie schooners and perhaps act as master mechanic during the five or six months in Chicago. Are you available to do this?

Also in case you are wouldn't it be better to build these wagons in Chicago in place of out here.

I would thank you to also advise me your lowest salary. I would want these schooners built very rought and as cheaply as they will only be used not to exceed six months.

With best wishes, I am

Your friend,

G. W. Lillie

G. W. Lillie "Pawnee Bill"

Pawnee Bill letter to Bock inquiring about building prairie schooners—1933. Kenneth Farnum.

This gold watch fob, given to Harry Bock in 1921 by Gordon W. Lillie, has Buffalo Bill and Pawnee Bill embossed under their profiles on the front with the following inscription on the back: "To Rev. Harry Bock in early days known as Buckskin Bill a great factor in civilizing the American Indians from G.W. Lillie 'Pawnee Bill' 1921." Kenneth Farnum.

86. Crowds at opening. Benton, Ill. Oct. 26, 1903

Introduction to the Photographs

The Monday afternoon crowds attending the Pawnee Bill's Wild West Show, in Benton, Illinois on Oct. 26, 1903, contributed to make the final week of Gordon Lillie's sixteenth season on the road a successful end to a profitable year. The Billboard *magazine on November 14, 1903 reported "The wild west's closing day at Pana, Ill. Oct. 31, wound up one of the best weeks business of the season. Roodhouse, Ill. Wednesday, proved the banner stand of the week, and one of the biggest financial days of the season, as people were turned away in the afternoon, after all standing room was occupied, and the night house seats sold at a premium. The show shipped direct to winter quarters, Carnegie, Pa., a suburb of Pittsburgh, where preparations were made in advance to house the entire show."*

While the majority of the performers and personnel left for their respective homes, a maintenance crew was housed at Carnegie to build and repair equipment for the 1904 season for which Lillie had announced his intention of "Vastly enlarging the show in every way." Among those who wintered at Carnegie was Harry Bock. Among his personal effects he brought his camera, one of the simple roll film cameras developed in the 1890s, which had made photography available to amateurs of modest means. In Carnegie Harry continued his interest in photographing the people, equipment, and events of the show of which he was a part. Indeed, there is evidence that it was there where Bock completed his photographic work, as none are dated after 1903, and he soon became fully involved in the Southern Baptist Convention.

While the recognition of photographs as historical documents developed through the next eighty years, Harry Bock's works were in possession of the Farnum family of Manchester, Vermont. I was fortunate to be one of the first people to view the collection of negatives which the Farnums had cared for during that time. Immediately I was reminded of the German word "Zeitgeist" which means "the spirit of the time." These images truly evoke the spirit of the Wild West Show.

On hearing the story of how the Farnums acquired the collection, it was evident that Bock understood the documentary value of his work. The promotional materials with which the show attracted patrons alluded to the end of the era of the Wild West and promised "An instructive, true insight into the manners, customs, and habiliments of the peoples of the pioneer west." Bock, too, conveyed this in the manner with which he passed on his work: accompanied by his vision of what it represented, a view of a uniquely American experience, a spectacle of the conquest of the west depicted in a way that never really was and would never be again.

Gordon Lillie knew the American West had changed forever. He also saw changes developing in the entertainment business. In addition to increased pressure from rival tent shows, moving pictures were emerging as a competitor for America's entertainment dollar. Lillie planned to offer them more for that dollar. He had been preparing for the next season even before the 1903 tour was completed.

On October 17, The Billboard *reported, "Master mechanics, photographers, and architects have been busy the past week preparing designs for cars and wagons for the next season. Major Lillie will spring a surprise feature on the show world next season, but its nature will not be known until near opening date." The nature of this surprise feature was the addition of the "Great Far East Show" to the banner. Lillie had in the past decade already incorporated many of these Far East elements into his shows, especially the comparative skills of horsemen from the world over. So this was not so much a new addition as it was a new promotional angle, and promotion was paramount in procuring patrons to provide plaudits for the performers as well as provide profits for promoters' pockets. Such was the language of the colorful posters and heralds which the advance advertising crews dispersed throughout the regions ahead of the show in the days before its arrival.*

The herald was a printed folio sheet lithographed on the outside with vivid illustrations and crammed with flowery and informative text. Dexter Fellows, in his 1936 autobiography This Way To The Big Show, *describes these as "printed heralds in colored inks extolling the amazing prodigious, colossal, stupendous, wonders of the forthcoming show." These heralds tantalized the reader and heightened their expectations, which were often rooted less in the true accounts of life and conditions in the west, than in the pulp fiction accounts of Pawnee Bill which greatly exaggerated the Major's actual accomplishments as well as living conditions in the pioneer west. In truth it was the show's intention both to dispel and indulge these expectations.*

Dexter Fellows is acknowledged as the dean of tent show press agents. He began his career, which was to span nearly fifty years, in 1893 with Pawnee Bill's Historic Wild West. Because the needs of the show where different during its 1894 European tour, Fellows was not retained for the next season. In 1895 he joined the Buffalo Bill Show, and in 1904 he returned for a single season as press agent for Pawnee Bill's Wild West and Great Far East Show. The press agent was responsible for generating publicity for the show in local newspapers and trade organs such as The Billboard. *Today these press accounts provide us with period commentaries and anecdotes about the performers and performances.*

Equally useful and insightful are the route books published yearly following the season. These are in essence a diary of the day to day occurrences of the previous year's tour. Although the compilers could not locate route books for the years 1901-1904, those located for the years 1898-1900 give us an indication of the rigors and dangers which the personnel and performers encountered in the daily routine of the show. This routine typically involved nightly travel between locations, unloading the tons of equipment upon arrival, and preparing for the street parade through town to the lot which had been selected in advance. Here the huge canvas tents, lighting apparatus, the arena, and seating for thousands of patrons were erected for the afternoon show at 2 p.m. and the evening show at 8 p.m. Following the evening show the entire outfit was dismantled, loaded onto the wagons, and secured to the flatcars for the rail journey to the next town.

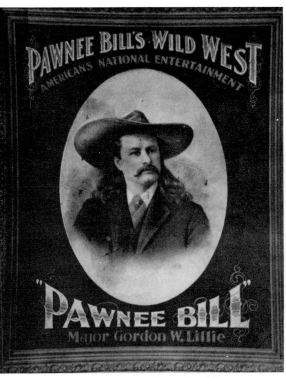

Front page of early 1900s Pawnee Bill herald—an example of his colorful hand-out advertising material. Circus World Museum.

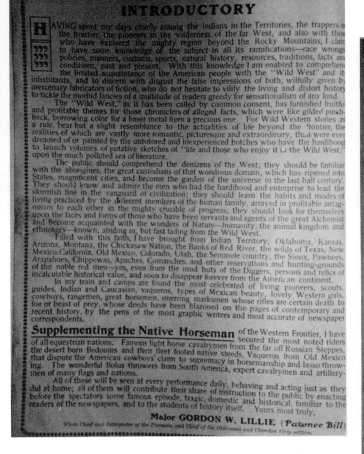

Page two of the herald extolling the virtues of Pawnee Bill. Circus World Museum.

Back page of herald—an excellent example of the color lithography then in use. Circus World Museum.

Page three of the herald describing the wonders of the untamed Wild west. Circus World Museum.

72. Unloading at Champlain, Ill.

The system which Lillie's crews employed to overcome the logistical complications of transporting the tons of equipment, as well as the dozens of performers and hundreds of horses, buffalo, and camels, was developed by the Buffalo Bill Show. Previously rail flatcars were loaded and unloaded from the side. Cody's system utilized a series of bridges between the flatcars. These were referred to in show accounts as "the Runs". By placing a ramp at the back of the train, the rolling stock was moved up the ramp and forward into place, and unloaded in the same manner. This innovation was observed by German military engineers during Buffalo Bill's European tours and incorporated into their military strategy for use in World War I.

The show's rolling stock was akin to today's containerized shipping. Each wagon was planned and designed to fulfil a specific purpose in Lillie's organization. Harry Bock's photographs illustrate the diversity of these wagons' designs and uses. Though Bock's images record the many facets of the shows activities, he seems to have had a special affinity for documenting the show's rolling stock. Perhaps this was because of his active participation in the creation of some of them. The evidence suggests that following his short lived attempt to launch his own "Buckskin Bill's Wild West Show," he rejoined Pawnee Bill's show just before or during its hiatus at Litchfield, Illinois for the winter of 1900-01.

It is there, apparently, that he began recording with his camera the images published here for the first time. It is likely that Harry supervised construction of the heavy utility wagons identified in his notes as having been constructed the following winter, the first of several spent at Carnegie, Pennsylvania. These include the mechanics wagon, canvas wagon, and the thirty-foot pole wagon. While these are examples of wagons designed strictly for utility, today we are most familiar with and indeed most intrigued by those which were designed to be beautiful as well as useful: those highly carved and colorfully decorated wagons which the show paraded through town as a final enticement to the populace to come and see the show.

39. Canvas wagon built at Carnegie, Pa. Season 1901-1902

16. #3 Band wagon, Pawnee Bill's W.W. Seasons 1896 to 1903

Gordon Lillie understood the advantages of this free preview which Americans had come to expect from traveling tent shows. A herald from the 1901 season calls attention to the "Weird and startling street parade" and implores the reader "Do not miss the strange and peculiar free exhibition that takes place in the morning of each show day." It further insists that " It is not a display of cheap finery, tawdry tinsel, or decrepit cage animals, but a vast assemblage of master horsemen of the world... Indians, warriors,...expert cowboy riders,...beautiful daring western girls." There are also references to "Australian boomerang throwers,....Japanese athletes, and Hindu fakirs." These are examples of Lillie's early interest in the Far East concept.

It is apparent that Lillie had been planning for the Far East show for some time. While the utilitarian wagons could be constructed by his own crews, the fancifully decorated show wagons were a product of specialty wagon makers. During his fifteen seasons through 1902, Pawnee Bill had amassed an impressive array of these bedazzling creations of the wainwright, including several large band wagons, and a number of diminutive pony wagons. In December, 1902, Lillie placed an order with the Sebastian Wagon Company for two more of these ornate wagons. The first was to be an immense band wagon, the other, described on the invoice as a "Japanese" wagon, was to augment the Far East theme. Today this original invoice survives to provide details of this transaction.

Founded by French immigrant Jacob Sebastian, the Sebastian Bros. Wagon Co. in New York City developed a reputation as one of the foremost makers of these elaborately decorated parade wagons. Jacob died in 1880 and the company continued under the supervision of his son John employing a specialized group of craftsmen, carpenters, and wheelwrights using oak and hickory to construct the sturdy framework to which were fastened the ornamental scrolls and figures executed by skilled carvers on thick planks and blocks of yellow pine, bass, and poplar. The whole was then embellished by artisans whose skills included figure painting, lettering, and gilding. The result was the epitome of the nineteenth century craft of the wainwright.

12. Japanese tableau wagon, Pawnee Bill's W.W. Season 1903

Arguably the finest surviving example of this firm's work is the band wagon commissioned by Major Lillie, now housed and maintained at the Circus World Museum in Baraboo, Wisconsin. Designed to carry an eighteen-piece band during parades, the carvings for this and the Japanese wagon were executed in the New York shops of Samuel A. Robb, where, in addition to these commissions for parade wagons, the studio's output included the familiar cigar store Indians, as well as a wide range of other show figures and trade carvings. The carved panels of the Pawnee Bill band wagon are an example of why Robb, today, is considered to have been in the front rank of American figure carvers of that era. One side is a depiction of the "Landing of Columbus" after the painting by John Vanderlyn (1775-1852), the other side represents Pocahontas saving the life of Captain John Smith of Jamestown. Equal skill is exhibited in the carved dragons and oriental figures of the Japanese Tableau wagon, the fate of which is unknown.

4. Larger view of the steam calliope

Lillie took delivery of these two wagons in the spring of 1903. It is likely that he also acquired the "Far East Tableau" wagon that same season. The visual impact of a procession of all these show pieces together was tremendously appealing to the spectator and the cacophony of sound which accompanied these parades served to reinforce the desire to attend the show: the tramp of hooves, the jangle of spurs, Indian war whoops, and above all the steam calliope. Yet, while all this equipment served its purpose in Lillie's show organization, it was the efficiency of his personnel which contributed most to his success and it was the skill and daring of his performers which the public was paying to see. Harry Bock photographed many of these people who were his co-workers and friends.

Bock's photographs of performers are both a portrait gallery of the players and a chronicle of their performances. Once again the heralds provide us with enticing and eloquent prose as an introduction to the players. While extolling the virtues of "Cowboy Character" it cautions the reader that "much has been written of the cowboy's prowess in the saddle and expertness with firearms, but little has been printed which does justice to his real character." It then chastises those "disreputable characters of all kinds in the west" who "adopted the dress, language, and general style of the cowboy in order to more easily accomplish their designs." Finally it reassures us that "The genuine American cowboy ... is a law abiding man, and the quickest and surest aid to the enforcement of the law when called upon by the authorities to hunt down bad men who are posing as cowboys."

The writer of The Billboard *"Notes from Pawnee Bill's Wild West" for October 3, 1903, credits some of the individual cowboys captured through Bock's lens. "Cowboys who are making a decided hit under the leadership of Eddie Botsford are... Harry Looms, Joe Casey, John McMaster, and Jack James, while the cowgirls received equally as much praise, Misses Lizzie Smart, Alice White, Winona Vonohl, Lulu Parr, and Adell Vonohl receiving rounds of applause daily."*

The cowgirls also received equal praise in the heralds, which told of those "Beautiful Daring Western Girls... Yes, the western girls can ride a horse, as you will readily perceive when you witness the performance of the bevy of Occidental Beauties with Pawnee Bill's Historical Wild West... There are many things worth seeing in Pawnee Bill's Historical Wild West, but not one prettier or more likely to be a gratifying afterthought in your memory than the lovely wild western girl with sparkling eyes and rosy cheeks who flashed by you on the back of a plunging steed."

The reality of this poetic vision of the plunging steed was that these women were subject to the same dangers as the cowboys and vaqueros. The heralds proclaimed them as "...some of the grandest horsemen in the world... They live in the saddle, but can get along without one. It is surprising to see them literally 'climb all over' a horse while it is careening at top speed over the plains. They can ride with equal security on its neck, beneath it, on either side, backward or forward and no steed can throw the vaquero." The Billboard notes "The Mexican rough riders, under command of Joseph Barras, Tiger Jack, Mexican Rufus, Jos Fernandez, and Don Zanana acquit themselves handsomely."

Unlike the other performers, the individual Indians are seldom identified in press accounts, but the writers of the heralds understood and capitalized on the public's curiosity and fascination with the Indians who in the perceptions of many were what had made the frontier west wild. For many the arrival of the show brought them their first look at these peoples whose former lands they now occupied. Harry Bock's portraits reflect the dignity of these proud men and women who might well have welcomed this chance to travel away from the reservations which were now their home. Among Bock's photographs of the performances, the Indians are represented in the Indian cremation dance and they are seen again in the attack on the prairie schooner.

This act climaxed with the cavalry detachment riding in to rescue the grateful travelers. This detachment was under the command of Jim Warren and was one of the topics of The Billboard "Notes" for October 17, 1903. "Captain James Warren and a detachment of cavalry are now performing one of the most applauded numbers of the show's program... The cavalry detachment now is as follows; Jas. G. Warren, Cpt. 6th cavalry; Frank Jones, 3rd cavalry; Courtney Hodges, 6th cavalry; Geo. Sullivan, 2nd cavalry; William Van Winkle, 2nd cavalry; George Vandeburg, 8th cavalry; Charlie Martin, 3rd cavalry... The horses as well as the trappings of the detachment are beautiful, and the artillery exercises and monkey drill received unstinted applause."

11A. Mexican Rufus

Lillie's contingent of Far East acts was providing a contrast to the Wild West performances. The audience's appetite for the exotic had been whetted on the midway of the side show. The colorfully painted banners invited them to an intriguing feast of curiosities, among them "The Big Footed Boy" who could be viewed for the token fee of a nickel. Another of Bock's views illustrates a precaution employed to protect those banners from the wind—still they attract the attention of those persons waiting to purchase tickets for the upcoming show. After availing themselves of the wares of the candy tent, the expectant patrons sought seating on the tiers of stringers in the Big House. Once seated, the audience was introduced to the performers during a ceremonial procession, after which they were dazzled by the diverse and daring display which was Pawnee Bill's Historic Wild West.

86A. Group of bosses

By all accounts Gordon Lillie was an astute businessman who appreciated the efforts of the crew of bosses who oversaw his operations. The contributions of several who were Harry Bock's subjects are noted in The Billboard *"Notes" for October 3, 1903: "Joseph Lynd and his two sons Ed and Will have charge of feeding everybody connected with the big Wild West and the cookhouse is pronounced by old timers to be one of the best in the business. Tom McAvoy and assistant Frank (Frenchy) Hall have broken all records in putting up and taking down the immense Wild West canvas. These two bosses pay about as much attention to rain and mud as a mallard duck."*

Another of Bock's photographs "Sledge gang" gives us a glimpse of some of the men responsible for McAvoy and Hall's success with the canvas. At the same time it illustrates the attention to detail and forethought which Harry seems to have applied in his compilation of these photographs. These behind-the-scenes snapshots have an impact beyond their pictorial content. Images such as "Camel with calf born in winter quarters...," "Buffalo watering at Champlain, Ill. Mexican Joe herding," and "Taking in the town from deck of stock car" convey the feeling of a casual glance over the shoulder at a private moment in the lives of the show people. This is a quality which enhances their obvious historical value.

Indeed, each photograph is a glance over the shoulder, that of Harry Bock, at that instant in time when the shutter of his carefully steadied camera opened to capture for the future another view of his world. In Bock's day the citizens of a community where the show pitched its tents for the day could approach the ticket wagon and for twenty-five or fifty cents experience this wondrous world of the Wild West Show. Today our ticket is the photographs of Harry Bock. Although each of Bock's images is but a black and white fragment of that world, collectively they convey much of the colorful pageantry of that now past part of Americana. Via his visionary views, we, too, can experience the amazing, prodigious, colossal, stupendous wonders of the Pawnee Bill Wild West Show.

12B. Lining up for parade

71. Section of train

68. Prairie schooner, ticket wagon, mechanical wagon, stage coach on car

69. Horses waiting at runs for wagons to be unloaded

74. Section of train.

76. Train

75. Taking in the town from deck of stock car.

66. First on the lot at Champlain, Ill.

89. Sledge gang

67. Indian camp and horse tent

5. Ticket wagon, Pawnee Bill's W.W.

77. Outside ticket seller

79. Kitchen and dining tent

35. Butcher wagon, Joe Lynd, prop., Pawnee Bill's W.W. Season 1901-1903

36. Refrigerator wagon, Pawnee Bill's W.W. Season 1901-1903

80. Windy day. Banners at half mast to avoid being torn by wind

82. Candy tent

81. View of side show and horse tents

85. Side show front

49. Tally ho coach 1900-03

100A. Introduction and line up. New and improved calcium lights hanging from poles provided the night time illumination.

98A. Grand entry

99A. Grand entry

73. Burros going on parade

8. *#1 Band wagon, Pawnee Bill's W.W. Season 1903.* The only known wagon from Pawnee Bill's Wild West directly traceable to the present is the twenty-one feet long by ten feet high red and gold Bandwagon #80, as it was known then in the Sebastian work-shop. Pawnee Bill used the wagon until 1909 when it went to the Mighty Haag Circus. In 1914 it went to the Miller Brothers, then from 1925 until 1930 it was used by the 101 Ranch Wild West Show. It was later acquired by the Bill Hames family and, in 1962, donated to the Circus World Museum. It can still be seen there in all its restored splendor!

6. Another view of the #1 Band wagon. Season 1903.

7. #1 Band wagon, Pawnee Bill's W.W. Season 1903

The author with the #1 (#80) bandwagon as it exists today at the Circus World Museum. Circus World Museum.

Front view of the #80 bandwagon. Circus World Museum.

Right side showing the hand-carved detail of the Landing of Columbus *after the painting by John Vanderlyn.* Circus World Museum.

69

Left side detail showing Pocahontas Saving the Life of Captain John Smith. Circus World Museum.

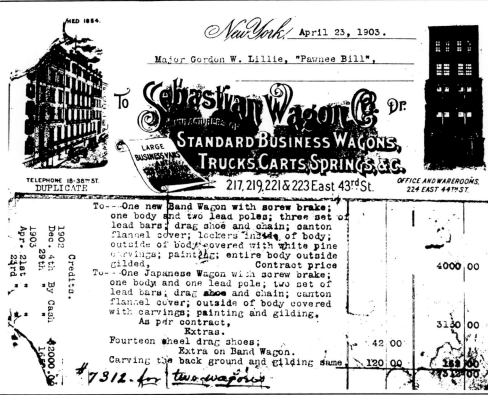

Bill of sale for #1 Bandwagon (#80) and Japanese Wagon constructed at the Sebastian Wagon Company in 1903. Circus World Museum.

Rear detail of the Pawnee Bill bandwagon. Circus World Museum.

15. #2 Band wagon, Pawnee Bill's W.W. Season 1893

17. #3 Band wagon, Pawnee Bill's W.W. Seasons 1896 to 1903

20. Side show band wagon, Pawnee Bill's W.W. Seasons 1896 to 1903

18. Mechanical organ wagon, Pawnee Bill's W.W. Season 1903

19. Far East tableau wagon, Pawnee Bill's W.W. Season 1903

21. Concert talent wagon, Pawnee Bill's W.W. Seasons 1899 to 1903

1. Chandelier wagon, Pawnee Bill's Wild West Season 1903. Taken at Watkins, N.Y.

90. Chandelier wagon going on parade

3. Steam calliope of the Pawnee Bill Wild West Season 1903. Taken at Carnegie, Pa.

50. Detail of front of steam calliope, Pawnee Bill's W.W. 1903

38. Stringer wagon built in winter quarters, Carnegie, Pa.

41. 30 ft. pole wagon built at Carnegie, Pa. Season 1901-1902

42. Reserved seat stringer wagon

37. Water wagon, Pawnee Bill's W.W. Season 1901-1903

13. Japanese tableau wagon, Pawnee Bill's W.W. Season 1903

22. Pony tableau, Pawnee Bill's W.W. Season 1895 to 1903

23. Pony tableau, Pawnee Bill's W.W. Season 1900-1903

24. Pony wagon, Pawnee Bill's W.W. Season 1901-1903

25. Pony wagon, Pawnee Bill's W.W. Season 1900-1903.

26. Pony wagon built in winter quarters, Litchfield. Ill. Season 1900-1901

27. Pony wagon built in winter quarters, Litchfield, Ill. Season 1900-1901

28. Pony prairie schooner built in winter quarters, Litchfield, Ill. Season 1900-1901

29. Group of pony wagons, Pawnee Bill's W.W. Season 1903

32. Pawnee Bill's private carriage, Chas. Metius driver, N. Nicodemus inside. Season 1902

33. Pawnee Bill's carriage. Season 1902

85A. Joe Lynn

51. Buffalo watering at Champlain, Ill. Mexican Joe (Jose Barrera) herding 1902

63. Baby camel and keeper. Born in winter quarters, Carnegie, Pennsylvania, 1903

64. Baby and camels. Pawnee Bill's Wild West and Far East, 1903.

82A. King Bill, boomerang thrower (Australia)

84A. Chandelier Blacky with the calcium lights that hung on poles for night performances.

87A. Tom McAvoy. He was canvas boss in charge of the main tents.

88A. Frenchy (Frank Hall) and Weston

89A. Tim

18A. Cowboys

13A. J. McMasters

14A. Mexicano. Hilario Cerrillo

15A. Jack James

103

16A. *Jerry Thompson.* He was also a jack knife wood carving expert in one of the side show tents.

20A. *Joe Casey,* cowboy

19A. *Ed Botsford.* He later spent time with Buffalo Bill and then joined the 101 Ranch Show.

33A. *Jim Warren.* He was photographer Harry Bock's best friend.

34A. *Jim Warren (*Captain James G. Warren, 6th Cavalry*)*

21A. *Cowboys.* Occasionally they were Indians doubling in the show or parade as cowboys.

31A. (William) Van Winkle, (George) Vanderberg, (Joseph) Casey, (George) Sullivan, Jim Warren

30A. Jim Warren and U.S. Monkey drill

78. *Horseshoer ready for business*

44. *Mechanical dept. H. Bock master mechanic, J. Bowers wagonsmith, T. James horseshoer*

108 *43. Mechanics wagon built at Carnegie, Pa 1901-02*

22A. Winona (Vonohl). Also known as Lillian Smith, she ended her career as a side-show attraction with the 101 Ranch show.

24A. Lulu Parr. She appeared with several other Wild West shows and also made a name for herself in the early rodeos.

23A. Edna May

26A. *H.(Harry) Loomis and girl* (Miss Lonnie)

28A. *Mrs. (Alice) White*

27A. *Amy McAvoy* in one of the Roman chariots specially made for the new Far East show.

40A. Eagle Bird and son

44A. Brave Bull

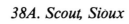

38A. Scout, Sioux

45A. Dog Horn

47A. Swift

46A. Helen White Hawk

56A. *Good Deer, Bad Wolf. Sioux*

52A. **Blue Horse and Boat Nail**

57A. *Johny Dog Ear. Sioux* **113**

63A. Iron Shell. Sioux

58A. Iron Shell, Henry Iron Shell, Crow Good Voice. Sioux

17A. Bucking horse. Tiger Jack, rider

94. Hanging the horse thief. Bock seems to have mislabeled this photograph. On close inspection it is the Arab acrobats.

84. Big house with act on

91. Military drill

3B. Indian cremation dance

2B. Mexican Joe. Pony express

97A. Attack on prairie schooner

77A. Russian Cossacks

68A. *Arab acrobats.* The Ali Brothers: Sarafon, Abdallam, Ambark, Side, and Salam.

74A. Arab tumbler

119

Pawnee Bill billboard. Circus World Museum.

Pawnee Bill. 1898 Pawnee Bill Route Book. Circus World Museum.

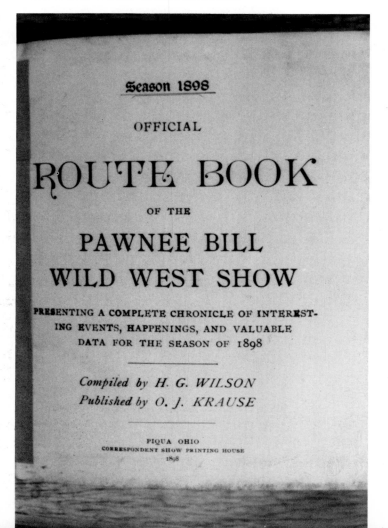

Title page of the 1898 Pawnee Bill Route Book with inside listing of Buckskin Harry Bock as both cowboy and carpenter. These small chronology books were published at the end of each season by most early tent shows. Circus World Museum.

MISS MAY LILLIE.
(World's Only Horse back Shot.)

May Lillie. 1898 Pawnee Bill Route Book. Circus World Museum.

PERSONNEL.

PAWNEE BILL'S HISTORIC WILD WEST.

General Winter Quarters . . . . Frederick, Md.
General Office . . . . . . 605 Sansom street, Philadelphia, Pa.

MANAGERIAL STAFF.

Maj. G. W. Lillie, (Pawnee Bill) . . . . Proprietor
O. J. Krause . . . . General Manager
H. W. Link . . . . General Agent
T. C. Howard . . . . Treasurer
H. G. Wilson . . . . Manager Privileges
W. E. Ferguson . . . . General Contracting Agent

PROFESSIONAL REPRESENTATIVES.

Butler C. Stewart, M. D. . . . . Chief Physician
Thos. E. Morrison . . . . Assistant Physician
James F. Sullivan . . . . Legal Representative

G. W. LINK.
(General Agent.)

Pages 8-9, 1898 Pawnee Bill Route Book. Circus World Museum.

PREFACE.

It is customary with the author of a book nowadays to start his pages with a preface. The author of this little volume will not deviate from this very good custom. It is with a pardonable feeling of pride that the author and publisher of this little record book places its pages before his friends and the public. Route books have come to be looked upon as an absolute necessity by the followers of the white tents. They afford a ready reference to events, furnish valuable data, and are frequently referred to in after years for interesting information. Every year witnesses an improvement in these little volumes. They grow more pretentious yearly, in order to keep pace with the great shows whose events they chronicle.

With the publication of this little book friends with the show, and others interested in circus affairs have a volume that it is hoped will afford them many a pleasant moment in perusing. It will freshen up many an incident that time has almost, if not quite, effaced from memory.

The author and publisher desires to take this opportunity to thank his numerous friends for their valuable assistance in helping him to collect the material for the pages that follow, and his most sincere hope is that it will give the reader as much pleasure as it has the author in compiling it. With these few words the book is submitted, hoping that its readers will deal gently in their criticism of any slight errors that might have crept into its pages.

O. J. KRAUSE.
(General Manager.)

Preface, 1898 Pawnee Bill Route Book. Circus World Museum.

FOREIGN OFFICE.

29 Strand . . . . London, England

DEPARTMENT SUPERINTENDENTS.

Heck Quinn . . . . Equestrian Director
Peter Sacketo . . . . Musical Director
R. B. Smith . . . . Proprietor Confectionery Dept.
H. G. Wilson . . . . Superintendent Annex
Frank Frost . . . . Press Agent
H. W. Mack . . . . Superintendent Outside Tickets
Butler C. Stewart, M. D. . . . . Principal Door Tender
James Sullivan . . . . Mail Agent
Chas. White . . . . Pinkerton Detective
C. E. Browne (succeeded by Chas. Williams) . . . . . .
. . . . Publisher of Programme
Chas. Bolus . . . . Superintendent Canvas
Chas. Evans . . . . Superintendent Stock
Jack Kent . . . . Superintendent Transportation
Doc Hinman . . . . Superintendent Cooking Department

ADVANCE CORPS OF PAWNEE BILL'S
WILD WEST.

H. W. Link . . . . . General Agent and Railroad Contractor
W. E. Ferguson . . . . General Contracting Agent
H. B. Hollis . . . . . Assistant General Contracting Agent
E. H. Danley . . . . Press Agent

MAJOR T. C. HOWARD.
(Treasurer.)

Pages 10-11, 1898 Pawnee Bill Route Book. Circus World Museum.

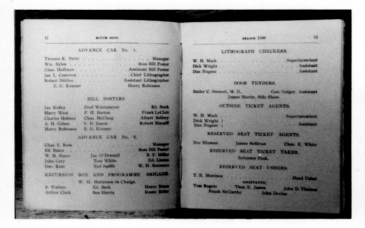

Pages 12-13, 1898 Pawnee Bill Route Book. Circus World Museum.

Pages 16-17, 1898 Pawnee Bill Route Book. Circus World Museum.

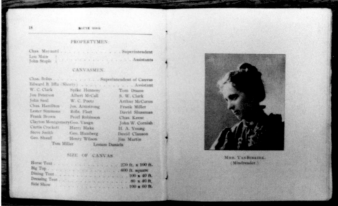

Pages 18-19, 1898 Pawnee Bill Route Book. Circus World Museum.

Pages 20-21, 1898 Pawnee Bill Route Book. Circus World Museum.

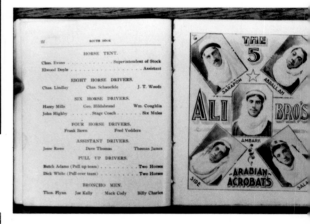

Pages 22-23, 1898 Pawnee Bill Route Book. Circus World Museum.

Pages 24-25, 1898 Pawnee Bill Route Book. Circus World Museum.

Pages 26-27, 1898 Pawnee Bill Route Book. Circus World Museum.

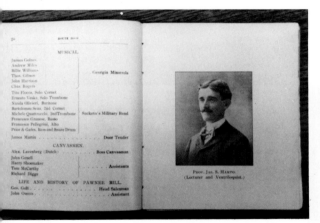

Pages 28-29, 1898 Pawnee Bill Route Book. Circus World Museum.

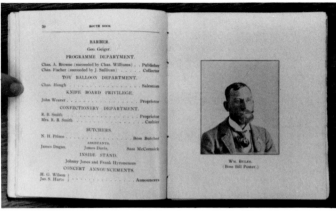

Pages 30-31, 1898 Pawnee Bill Route Book. Circus World Museum.

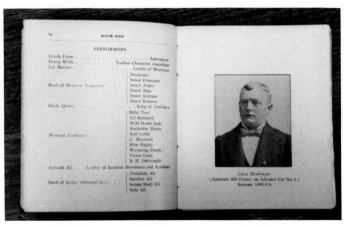

Pages 34-35, 1898 Pawnee Bill Route Book. Circus World Museum.

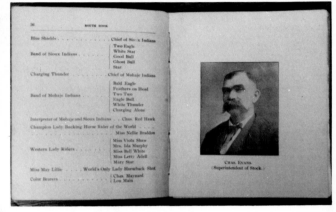

Pages 36-37, 1898 Pawnee Bill Route Book. Circus World Museum.

Pages 38-39, 1898 Pawnee Bill Route Book. Circus World Museum.

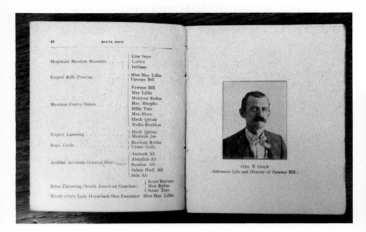

Pages 40-41, 1898 Pawnee Bill Route Book. Circus World Museum.

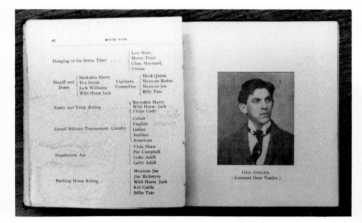

Pages 42-43, 1898 Pawnee Bill Route Book. Circus World Museum.

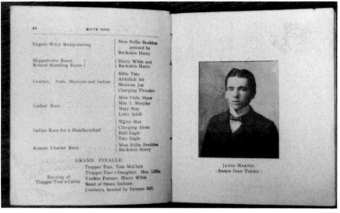

Pages 44-45, 1898 Pawnee Bill Route Book. Circus World Museum.

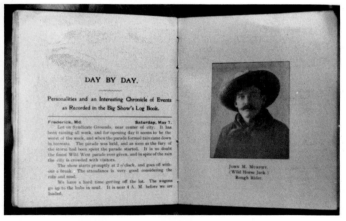

Pages 46-47, 1898 Pawnee Bill Route Book. Circus World Museum.

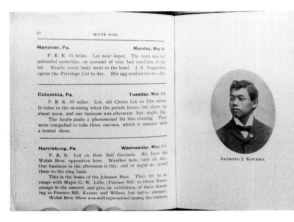

Pages 48-49, 1898 Pawnee Bill Route Book. Circus World Museum.

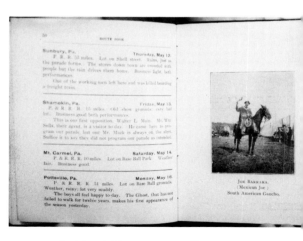

Pages 50-51, 1898 Pawnee Bill Route Book. Circus World Museum.

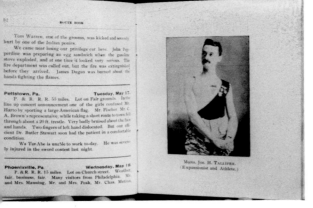

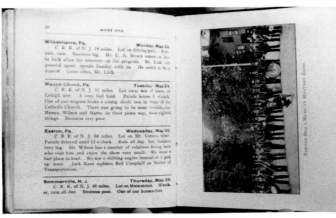

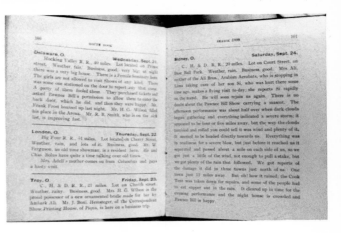

Pages 52-53, 1898 Pawnee Bill Route Book. Circus World Museum.

Pages 56-57, 1898 Pawnee Bill Route Book. Circus World Museum.

Pages 100-101, 1898 Pawnee Bill Route Book. Circus World Museum.

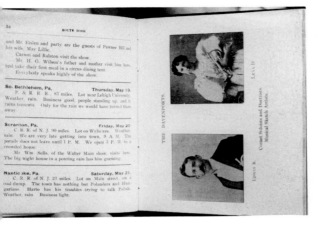

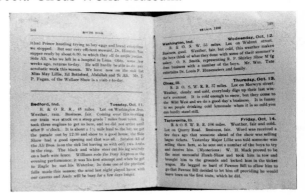

Pages 54-55, 1898 Pawnee Bill Route Book. Circus World Museum.

Pages 108-109, 1898 Pawnee Bill Route Book. Circus World Museum.

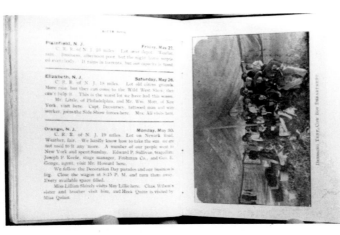

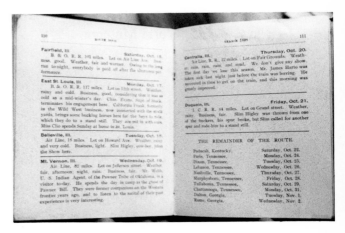

Pages 58-59, 1898 Pawnee Bill Route Book. Circus World Museum.

Pages 110-111, 1898 Pawnee Bill Route Book. Circus World Museum.

"Tent Shows" columns from The Billboard, *show business magazine. October 3 and October 17, 1903.* Circus World Museum.

OCT. 3, 1903

OCT. 17, 1903

NOV. 14, 1903

ROUTES AHEAD.

The Billboard forwards mail to all professionals free of charge. Members of the professions are invited while on the road to have their mail addressed in care The Billboard and it will be promptly forwarded.

"Tent Shows" column and advertising from The Billboard, *show business magazine. November 14, 1903.* Circus World Museum.

Epilogue

Researchers are familiar with the limitations of time and expense in a thorough search and examination of pertinent data on a given subject. In an effort to enrich the historical legacy of Harry Bock's remarkable images, we are extending an invitation to the reader to contribute to the continuing efforts of the compilers to locate additional materials which relate to the lives and work of Harry Bock and Gordon Lillie. We are seeking letters, diaries, photographs, promotional items, news accounts, and artifacts of any of the employees and performers—before, during, and after their involvement with the Wild West show.

Address your commentaries, criticisms, and data contributions to the author or research assistant at Aldor Enterprises, P.O. Box 7078-Hollywood Station, Salem, OR 97303.

Elephant poster for the Two Bills show, 1910 or 1911. Circus World Museum.

Two Bills poster from around 1910. Circus World Museum.

Bibliography

Berkshire Courier, Great Barrington, Massachusetts. Bock obituary October 20, 1949.

Billboard, The. Show business magazine, New York. Tent Shows and route columns covering the period 1895-1905.

Birches Funeral Home, Great Barrington, Massachusetts. Bock file.

Burke, John. *Buffalo Bill, The Noblest Whiteskin*. G. P. Putnam's Sons, New York 1973.

Chatham Courier, Chatham, NY. Bock headlines October 13, 1949.

Circus World Museum, Baraboo, Wisconsin. Owned by the State Historical Society of Wisconsin. Pawnee Bill/Buffalo Bill/Buckskin Bill Wild West posters, photographs, couriers, heralds, programs, route books, misc. files 1888-1913.

Cody, Colonel William F. *An Autobiography of Buffalo Bill*. Holt, Rinehart and Winston, Inc. 1920. Winchester Press, New York 1969.

Daily Free Press, Beloit, Wisconsin. Column of July 27, 1901.

Daily World, Tulsa, Oklahoma. Story about Pawnee Bill in Sect. 4, December 31, 1933.

Farnum, Kenneth. Great Barrington, Massachusetts. Bock family history, photographs, and memorabilia.

Farnum, Lester Fayette (1880-1970), Manchester Depot, Vermont. Collection of old Bock photographs.

Federated Church of Athens, New York. Bock ministering history, 1943-1949.

Lillie, Gordon William (Pawnee Bill). *Major Gordon W. Lillie's Own Story*. Unpublished manuscript written with L. M. Sullivan in Kansas City, possibly 1937.

Mark Skinner Library, Manchester, Vermont. Photographs and records of Bock family.

New York Department of Health, Albany. Vital records.

Pawnee Bill Museum, Oklahoma Tourism and Recreation Department, Pawnee, Oklahoma. Photographs and historical material.

Russell, Don. *The Wild West*. Amon Carter Museum of Western Art, Fort Worth, Texas 1970.

———— *The Lives and Legends of Buffalo Bill*. University of Oklahoma Press, Norman 1960.

———— *The Golden Age of Wild West Shows*. Article in Westerners Brand Book, February 1970.

Shirley, Glenn. *Pawnee Bill*. University of New Mexico Press 1958. Bison reprint, University of Nebraska Press 1965.

Southern Baptist Convention, The Historical Commission of. Nashville, Tennessee. Yearbooks, records, and publications.

Town Clerk, Manchester, Vermont. Vital statistics and old records.

U. S. Census 1910. Bennington County, Southern Vermont, Pg.4331.

Western History Collection, University of Oklahoma, Norman. Photographs and historical material.

World. *How Pawnee Bill Rode In*. New York newspaper clipping May 5, 1889.